We Planted Seeds Today

ISBN 978-1-0980-6115-9 (paperback)
ISBN 978-1-0980-6117-3 (digital)

Christian Faith Publishing, Inc.
832 Park Avenue
Meadville, PA 16335
www.christianfaithpublishing.com

Printed in the United States of America

We Planted Seeds Today

Benita Elcock

Today Daddy and I are going to plant squash seeds.

"First, Daddy gathered all of the eggshells Mommy saved for us."

Then Daddy let me put a teaspoon of soil inside each eggshell. Boy, was it fun. It got a little messy!

After that, we placed a seed in the center of
the soil, in each slot of the egg carton.
Daddy reminded me to cover the seeds with soil!

We then watered each slot to make sure the soil was moist.

The next thing we did was place the egg carton in the window seal so it could get plenty of sunlight.

We were sure to look in on them and water them every day.

Mommy even said we should sing to them!

"Mmmm-hmmmm…Mmmm-hmmmm."

After a few days, we saw them sprout.

Each day they grew taller, with leaves spreading wide.

Daddy decided to take them out.
He went in the garden and dug a hole, leaving
space in between for the squash to grow!

Before we knew it, squash was all about.

Message from the Author

Planting seeds in our children, nurturing them and watching them grow, has been the most magical experience.

About the Author

"Benita Elcock is a wife and a mother of two. She takes joy in being with her family. She's a dreamer that realizes that in every moment, we're either learning or teaching and, in some cases, we're at an interesting crossroad where the two meet. She loves to teach and inspire her children, and has realized just how much her children have taught and inspired her as well."

CPSIA information can be obtained
at www.ICGtesting.com
Printed in the USA
BVHW022245260622
640644BV00004B/26